LIFE IN THE
POLAR LANDS

Author: **Monica Byles**

Consultant: Roger Hammond,
Director of Living Earth

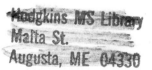
WORLD BOOK / TWO-CAN

Published in the United States and Canada in 1997 by
World Book, Inc.
525 W. Monroe
20th Floor
Chicago, IL USA 60661
in association with Two-Can Publishing Ltd.

**For information on other World Book products,
call 1-800-255-1750, x 2238.**

ISBN: 0-7166-5206-4 (hbk.)
ISBN:0-7166-5207-2 (pbk)
LC: 96-61735

Text and design by Monica Byles

Printed in Hong Kong

1 2 3 4 5 6 7 8 9 10 01 00 99 98 97

Photograph credits:
p.4 (top) NHPA/Stephen Kraseman p.4/5 NHPA/Gordon Claridge p.7 Survival Anglia/Joel Bennett p.8 Ardea/Clem Haagner p.10 (top) Survival Anglia/Rick Price (bottom) B. & C. Alexander p.11(top) Ardea (bottom) Ardea/Jean-Paul Ferrero p.12 Ardea/E. Mickleburgh p.13 (top) Ardea/Ron & Valerie Taylor (bottom) NHPA/Stephen Kraseman p.14 Bruce Coleman/Inigo Everson p.15 (top) Survival Anglia/Rick Price (bottom) Ardea/François Gohier p.16 B. & C. Alexander p.19 Bruce Coleman/Norbert Rosling p.20/21 Survival Anglia/Colin Willcock p.21 Bruce Coleman/E. & P.Bauer p.22 NHPA/Peter Johnson p.23 B. & C. Alexander/Robert Estall Front cover: Seaphot/Planet Earth/Howard Platt Back cover: Tony Stone Worldwide

Illustrations by Francis Mosley. Edited by Claire Watts. Artworking by Claire Legemah.

CONTENTS

LOOKING AT THE POLES

Few areas in the world are as harsh and desolate as the North and South poles, and few are as beautiful. For much of the year both areas are freezing cold, with fierce winds and thick snow and ice on the ground. As it grows colder even the seas freeze.

Not many animals live here. Some species, however, are hardy enough to live, breed, and find food in the open wastes. Their bodies have specially adapted to the constant cold.

In the summer months, May to July at the North Pole and November to January at the South Pole, the sun shines even at midnight. In winter, the poles remain almost permanently dark.

The snow and ice recede in the short summers, leaving the ground littered with pools of **meltwater**. The land is covered with flowers and bursts of green leaves. Creatures mate and nest or find safe places to give birth to their young. The air is filled with insects.

▶ Plants in the polar lands spend most of the time under snow but burst into life during the short summer. Their seeds are very hardy and do not **germinate** until the conditions around them are exactly right for growth.

▼ A large **iceberg** floats in the summer sea off Antarctica. It is sunset, but at this time of year the sky never really grows dark.

WHERE IN THE WORLD?

The poles are at the top and bottom of the earth. Because they are farther from the sun than any other point on earth, the sun's rays are weaker, which makes the polar lands colder than anywhere else in the world.

At the North Pole lies a frozen sea, called the Arctic Ocean. This ocean is surrounded by Europe, Asia, and North America. The most northerly point where trees will grow is about 1,429 miles (2,300 kilometers) from the North Pole. Between the **tree line** and the **icecap** lie regions of **tundra**, which is rough terrain covered with rugged vegetation. The layer of earth beneath the tundra is always frozen, even in summer. It is called **permafrost**.

The continent of Antarctica lies at the South Pole and is permanently covered in **ice sheets** known as the Antarctic icecap.

HISTORY OF THE POLES

150-170 million years ago

The poles are not frozen. The South Pole may lie over low ground and the North Pole over open ocean.

60-70 million years ago

Shifts in the earth's plates cause the poles to move to the positions where they now lie. They begin to cool.

5-6 million years ago

The polar lands are still quite warm at sea level. Changes in the climate and in the heat received from the sun bring new conditions of snow and ice, which have been there ever since.

NORTH POLE FACTS

● Because the North Pole is surrounded by land, warmer currents from close to the equator never reach the Arctic Ocean to warm it.

● The ancient Greeks named the Arctic after the constellation of the Great Bear, which they called Arktos.

● Americans Robert Peary and Matthew Henson were the first explorers to reach the North Pole in 1909.

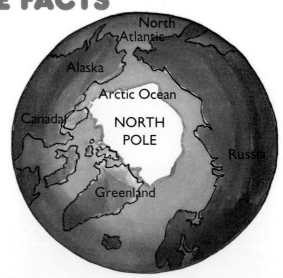

Snow and ice lie deeper here than anywhere else in the world.

The poles were not always such cold places. Fossils of trees, plants, and dinosaurs found in Antarctica show that it once had a much warmer climate. Movements of the **plates** that make up the earth's surface, together with the

▲ A herd of caribou passes along the northern treeline on its annual journey to richer feeding grounds.

warming and cooling of our planet over many centuries, have finally brought about the chilly conditions we know at the poles today.

SOUTH POLE FACTS

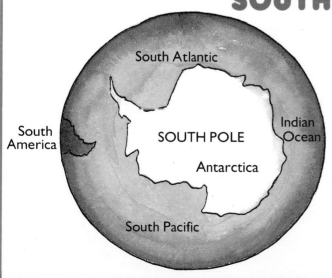

South Atlantic

South America

SOUTH POLE

Indian Ocean

Antarctica

South Pacific

● Seventy-five percent of the world's water is stored in glaciers, and most of this lies in the Antarctic icecap.

● The Antarctic can be called a desert, as it receives less than 6 inches (150 millimeters) of rain or snow per year.

● Norwegian Roald Amundsen beat Britain's Robert Scott to the South Pole by five weeks in 1911.

FROZEN FEATURES

One-fourth of the world's oceans and seas are affected by ice every year. Most of this comes in the form of icebergs. An Antarctic iceberg has reached almost as far as Rio de Janeiro, a journey of 3,440 miles (5,500 kilometers).

At the South Pole, ice covers the land and forms cliffs and **glaciers**. As the ice in the glaciers becomes old and heavy, it moves slowly forward and reaches the sea after many years. Long tongues of this glacier extend out into the sea, and large chunks of ice break off. This ice floats away to become new icebergs.

◀ Paradise Bay Glacier in the Antarctic. Sections break off from these craggy cliffs and plummet into the clear waters below to form new icebergs.

Icebergs are made from frozen fresh water, but at the poles the salty ocean freezes, too. This reaches a peak in February and March, when there is about 4.5 million square miles (12 million square kilometers) of sea ice in the Arctic Ocean and 1 million square miles (3 million square kilometers) off Antarctica.

As the sea freezes, a greasy film appears to cover the water. A curtain of wispy "smoke" rises from the surface and, as the seawater turns to ice, salt is pushed above the surface in beautiful crystals called **ice flowers**.

Ever since the sinking of the ocean liner the Titanic by an iceberg in 1912, in which 1,517 lives were lost, the International Ice Patrol has kept watch on icebergs to alert ships to possible danger in the ocean.

DIFFERENT KINDS OF ICE

● As the sea freezes, the first ice to form is not very solid. It is called **frazil ice**. As the salt content is pushed out, thick **pancake ice** forms. Finally slabs of ice freeze together to form **pack ice**.

● Glacier bergs have broken off glaciers that run into the sea. This is dense, ancient ice. As it is so heavy, only about one-tenth shows above the water's surface.

● **Tabular icebergs** have broken off from ice shelves. They have flat tops and are sometimes used by scientists as convenient research bases.

● Fragments of ice are called **brash ice**. Large fragments from the **icecap** are called **bergy bits**, and smaller pieces are known as **growlers**.

ANIMAL LIFE

Despite the bleakness of the polar lands, many animals live there, either all year around or as summer visitors when the temperature rises to 50°F (10°C) above freezing.

On the Antarctic icecap most of the permanent residents are insects. On the very edge of the ice there are penguins, seals, and migratory birds, while the sea is filled with an abundance of life.

An enormous variety of animals live in the Arctic, from the tiny shrew to the huge polar bear. Native species are well adapted to make use of the short summer and protect themselves against the long winter. Polar animals tend to be larger than their cousins in warmer climates. They have short legs, long hair, and an undercoat of dense

▲ The stoat, like many other animals grows a white **pelt** during the winter. This helps to **camouflage** it against the snow when it hunts.

▼ Polar bear cubs are born in pairs and stay with their mother for up to 2 years. Polar bears may live up to 33 years in the wild.

▶ Seals come in many shapes and sizes. They are superbly adapted to life in and out of water. Seals are torpedo-shaped to help them glide easily through the water. Their bodies are covered in a thick layer of **blubber**, which protects their internal organs from the cold. This blubber is between 1 and 6 inches (2.5 and 15 centimeters) thick and gives seals energy when there is no food available.

fur. Their tails are short, and the pads on their large feet are furry.

Every 10 to 13 years small mammals such as lemmings or voles breed in enormous numbers. With such a ready supply of food available, larger meat-eaters also grow in number. Eventually there is little vegetation for the small mammals to eat, and many of them die. The larger animals then also suffer a large population drop, and the vegetation begins to grow back.

◀ A pack of wolves follows its leader into the treeline. A wolf can see and smell its prey more than 1 mile (1.6 kilometers) away. Most wolves have gray fur, but the Arctic wolf may grow pure white fur for camouflage against the snow.

Wolves can eat up to 20 pounds (9 kilograms) of food at one time. However, they can go without eating for two weeks or longer.

BIRDLAND

The polar winter is too cold for most birds. But during the summer many species of birds arrive. The Arctic tern flies from summer at one pole to summer at the other. It covers a distance of 18,750 miles (30,000 kilometers) every year. Other birds include geese, ducks, and smaller birds such as larks and pipits. On the surface lie pools of melted ice and snow where millions of mosquitoes and other insects flourish. The humming air is a feast for birds!

During the winter, a number of birds live on the **subarctic** wastes of the tundra, where they live by searching for roots and berries under the snow or by feeding on other birds, small mammals, or insects. Here in the north live the ptarmigan, the snowy owl, and, close to the tree line, the raven and Arctic redpoll.

Throughout the Antarctic year, birds such as penguins remain hardy in all conditions. A penguin can dive as deep as 164 feet (50 meters) underwater in search of fish. This is the height of a 24-story building! King penguins must return to land every five to six weeks during the winter to feed their growing young. The adults then cluster together on the shore. The cold penguins from the edge of the group exchange places with the warmed birds from the center every few minutes. Their young soon grow into enormous brown furry lumps of some 26 pounds (12 kilograms) in body weight but have to fast for up to a month at a time while their parents are out at sea. By the spring they weigh no more than 13 pounds (6 kilograms). Many chicks die during this period.

◀ The largest of the penguin family is the Emperor. It stands more than 3 feet (1 meter) tall and weighs up to 90 pounds (40 kilograms). The male penguin **incubates** the eggs in a special pouch on his feet. He will go as long as two months without eating.

▲ A black-browed albatross flies over the Antarctic Ocean. It has long, thin wings, which help it to glide through the air.

▼ Puffins fly to the Arctic during the summer and nest among the rocky cliffs surrounding the frozen ocean.

SEA LIFE

Below the waves and ice of the polar oceans, the temperature remains far more constant than at the surface. For this reason, creatures such as polar bears, seals, and penguins prefer to spend as much time as possible diving and swimming.

In the Antarctic the stable temperature and warm currents from more temperate zones encourage many varieties of colorful growth. Bright orange sea spiders, delicate anemones, fronds of primitive weeds, worms, and other strange creatures litter the sea floor.

Strange ghostly fish live here, too, like the pale ice-fish or transparent deep-sea angler. In areas under the ice where little light filters through to

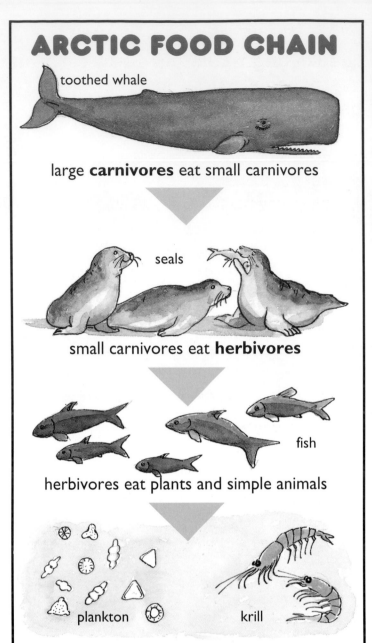

ARCTIC FOOD CHAIN

toothed whale

large **carnivores** eat small carnivores

seals

small carnivores eat **herbivores**

fish

herbivores eat plants and simple animals

plankton   krill

This is a food chain of polar animals living in the sea. Smaller animals tend to be eaten by larger animals. Herbivores eat only plants or simple life such as krill. At the bottom of the chain, plants and simple animals do not need to eat major organisms to stay alive.

◀ Krill are tiny crustaceans similar to shrimp. Some countries, including Japan, have recently begun fishing for krill to provide food for people. This mass harvesting of krill poses a threat to the creatures of polar lands, which rely on them as a primary food source.

the depths, these creatures have no need of bright coloring. Many carry an internal light source, supplied by bacteria carried in a special gland.

The largest marine animals, the whales, live mainly in the Antarctic. Biggest of all are the blue whales, which grow up to 98 feet (30 meters) long and weigh 14.8 tons (150,000 kilograms). They are the largest animals on earth. There are two groups of whales: **toothed whales**, which feed on fish and seals, and **baleen whales**, which feed on tiny creatures called krill. Baleen whales have a series of bony plates in their mouths, which helps them sift the krill from the water.

▶ This killer whale is breaching. Killer whales are members of the dolphin family. They can swim as fast as 25 miles per hour (40 kilometers per hour). They swim in all oceans but prefer polar waters.

◀ This giant sea spider has 10 legs. It lives on the ocean floor near the South Pole. Sea spiders have between 4 and 10 legs. They are not members of the same family group as land spiders, all of which have 8 legs.

The bodies of sea spiders are so small that some of the spiders' food is digested in their legs!

PEOPLE OF THE POLES

On the icecap of Antarctica there are no human residents. Only scientists brave these regions to carry out their experiments.

In the Arctic, however, local peoples have learned how to survive in the harsh climate. Many still live as **nomads**, following the herds of animals that provide their livelihood, although today many of them have a fixed home in one of the settlements.

The Inuit, or Eskimo as they are sometimes known, live in North America and Russia and are the largest group. Few still drive sleds

▼ Igloos are now mostly built as overnight resting places on long hunting trips. They are built from large slabs of ice, carefully cut to size and placed together for a snug fit against the winds. Traditional lighting came from whale or seal oil burned in a small container. This also efficiently heated the room.

pulled by husky dogs or wear the traditional stitched animal skins. Most prefer to ride over the icecap on engine-driven snowmobiles and to wear anoraks; although the stitched skins are, in fact, even warmer.

Today the closely related Inuit tribes of Alaska and Russia are allowed to meet without regard to political boundaries. Changes in the way Eastern Europe is governed mean that people living there are able to visit other countries more freely than under the old laws.

The people of the North may in the future find it easier to fish and hunt where the animals wander and not where governments force them to live.

PEOPLE FACTS

● The Yahgans and Onas, who used to live in the Antarctic region at the tip of South America, have died out.

● Arctic people eat mostly fish and meat, as there is little plant life available.

● More than 100,000 Inuit are spread over four countries along the Arctic coastline.

▲ An Inuit man wearing his traditional costume of boots, leggings, trousers, hooded jacket, and mitts. These are made from the skins of animals such as caribou, bear, or wolf. The clothes are made loose-fitting to allow an extra layer of warm air around the body. The seams are tightly sewn to waterproof the garment.

WATCHING THE WEATHER

Polar lands are useful places to study the weather, because the temperature at the poles affects climates all over the world. It is the cold air blowing from the poles and meeting the hot air from the equator that causes our weather patterns. Scientists can also find out about patterns in the world's climate that existed thousands of

▼ This map shows major cities around the world that will be in serious danger of being submerged by the sea if the polar icecaps melt as a result of global warming. Even world centers such as London or New York would be lost beneath the waters.

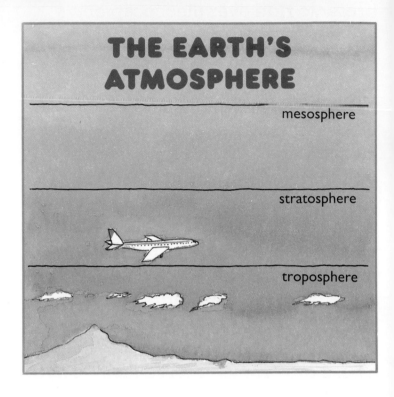

THE EARTH'S ATMOSPHERE

mesosphere

stratosphere

troposphere

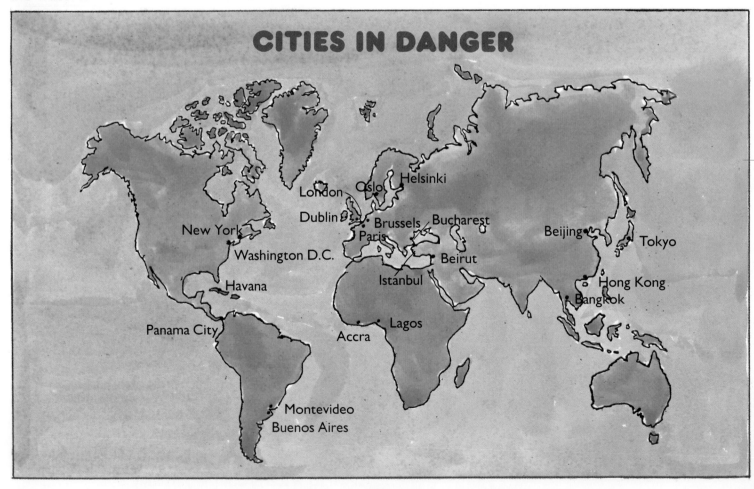

CITIES IN DANGER

Helsinki
Oslo
London
Dublin
Brussels   Bucharest
New York   Paris
Washington D.C.   Beirut
Havana   Istanbul
Panama City   Lagos
Accra
Beijing
Tokyo
Hong Kong
Bangkok
Montevideo
Buenos Aires

years ago by studying the ice that has lain at the poles since that time.

The world is warming up for many reasons. Chief among these is the growing hole in the **ozone layer** at each pole, where it is thickest. This is the layer within the stratosphere layer of the earth's atmosphere that protects us from the sun's harmful ultraviolet rays. The ozone is being destroyed by human-made chemicals including chlorofluorocarbons (CFCs), which are used in aerosol sprays.

Global warming is also increased by the effect of **greenhouse gases**. Gases produced by industrial processes are building up in the earth's atmosphere. These gases act as a blanket, trapping

▲ The aurora borealis is a beautiful and rare sight seen mainly near the North Pole. It is caused by the entry of solar particles into the earth's magnetic field. A similar phenomenon in the Antarctic is known as the aurora australis.

HOW YOU CAN HELP THE WORLD

● Give up using aerosol sprays which contain CFCs. Look out for alternatives that are now widespread in supermarkets. Most are pumps and are labeled "ozone friendly" or "CFC free."

● Ask adults to compost garden waste instead of burning it. Chemicals in the smoke pollute the atmosphere. And compost helps new plants to grow.

● Try to persuade adults to run their cars on leadfree gasoline. A car that runs on gasoline containing lead releases into the atmosphere its own weight in carbon dioxide fumes every year.

heat from the sun instead of allowing it to be reflected back into space.

As the world grows warmer, so the oceans around the poles grow more hospitable. At present, polar temperatures rise only to 50°F (10°C) at the very height of summer. If the temperature were to rise by more than five percent at the poles, the ice would melt and sea levels across the world could rise drastically. Low-lying cities such as London and New York as well as whole countries such as the Netherlands and Bangladesh could be flooded. At these temperatures many of the specialized animals and plants of the polar regions would die out, too.

EXPLOITING THE POLES

The first outsiders to see potential for making money in the poles came during the 1800's. They killed whales in great numbers for their meat and for their blubber, which was used in a variety of products from soap to oil. Seals, particularly fur seals, were trapped for their attractive pelts. Penguins were killed, because their oil was useful as a light source.

Today international agreements are in force to protect the creatures of the poles from hunters. A few animals are still killed each year for scientific purposes, and local peoples are also permitted to hunt and kill a number of animals.

Animals face other dangers, too. Polar bears are great scavengers and may become too dependent on scientific bases for scraps of food. They can often be seen in garbage dumps, where they sometimes eat unsuitable things, cut themselves on sharp edges, or lose the will to hunt.

Extra industrial activity at the poles may also add to the world's environmental problems. The glaring white surface of the icecap at each pole helps to reflect back into space hot rays from the sun.

Pale colors bounce rays off their surface. Bright, shiny snow is very good at doing this. Dark colors soak in warm rays of light and grow hotter. This is why you may prefer to wear light-colored clothes to help you stay cool in the hot summer.

POLAR RESOURCES

● Ninety-eight percent of Antarctica is covered by thick ice, but beneath may lie valuable deposits of rubies and other minerals.

● Reserves of oil and natural gas lie under Alaska, Arctic Canada, and Siberia. Further oil deposits are found off the coast of Greenland, on the Arctic shores of the North Atlantic, and in parts of the Antarctic Ocean.

● Oil spillage from a tanker accident in Alaska in the spring of 1989 killed many birds and other animals.

◀ The bleached-white bones of long-dead whales remind us of the years when these great mammals were hunted mercilessly. The bowhead whale was even called the "right" whale because it was so easy to catch.

▲ A polar bear forages among the discarded litter of a modern settlement in northern Canada. He could be poisoned or injured and also poses a serious threat to the local people.

Some scientists fear that dust and grime from industrial processes might make the ice darker, thereby reflecting fewer rays than at present. This would trap heat in the earth's atmosphere and increase the effects of global warming.

If people attempt to melt the permafrost to mine minerals and other resources, there may also be the danger that modern structures such as buildings, railroads, or vital oil-relaying pipelines will be ruined.

SAVING THE POLES

It is important that human beings realize the importance of keeping the polar lands clean for the future. The specialized animals and plants will die if the temperatures are allowed to rise.

Sensible measures have been taken to establish both the North and South poles as areas of special scientific interest rather than purely as areas to be exploited. The first legal restraint on animal slaughter in these regions was passed by Great Britain in 1904. Since then many other nations have joined to save threatened species.

The long-standing Antarctic Treaty concerning ownership of the lands of the South Pole was agreed upon by most of the world's governments.

Even industry has taken steps to avoid future damage to this most desolate of the world parks. Special ice roads have been built to protect slow-growing plants from being crushed under the wheels of a succession of heavy vehicles.

Similarly, oil and gas pipelines are built up off the ground like bridges. Despite people's continuing encroachment on the lands of the poles, the caribou in the North may continue their migration in peace.

▲ A rookery of King penguins shows the efficiency of creatures that have adapted to extreme conditions. If the poles become warmer, the penguins may not survive.

▶ An aerial view of the snow-crusted ridges of Greenland. The world would lose one of its great natural beauties if we allow the destruction of the polar icecaps.

CROW STEALS SOME DAYLIGHT

For thousands of years people have told stories about the world around them. Often these stories try to explain something that people do not really understand, like how the world began or where light comes from. This tale is told by the Inuit who live in the polar lands of northern Canada.

Long ago, in the northern lands where the Inuit live, there was no daylight. The people ate, slept, went hunting, and cooked all in darkness. There was no light to tell the people which was day and which was night, so they all got up at different times. When they needed to see they

day he told them about a land where light shone all day and people could see without using a lamp and could spot animals far off. The villagers were amazed at this and began to realize how difficult their lives were without light during the day.

would light little seal-oil lamps, which gave off a small glimmer of light, scarcely enough to see by.

In one village lived a wise old Crow. He used to tell the people stories of the far-off lands that he had visited. One

"When we go fishing," said one, "we have to shine a light into the holes we make in the ice to see if any fish are there, and that scares the fish off. If it were light all the time, we would be able to see the fish before they saw us."

24

"And without light," said another, "we are quite likely to walk straight into the arms of a polar bear before we even realize that it's there. If it were light all the time, we would be able to see polar bears in the distance and keep away."

All the villagers begged the Crow to go to the land of daylight and fetch them some light. At first the Crow said no, because it was such a long journey. But the villagers had always been very good to him, so eventually he agreed.

It was a very long journey indeed and when, at last, the Crow reached the eastern lands where the sky was bright with daylight, he sank to the ground, exhausted. He found himself in a village not so very different from the one he had left. In the middle of the village was a house from which daylight shone brightly.

"Aha!" thought the Crow. "That is where the daylight comes from."

As he watched, a woman walked up to the house. The Crow flew over to the door, shook off his skin, and turned himself into a speck of dust, which settled on the woman's dress as she went into the house.

Inside the house a great chief sat watching a baby playing on a fur rug. As the woman passed she bent down and tickled the baby. She didn't notice the tiny speck of dust fall from her dress and into the little baby's ear. It was the Crow of course!

The baby tugged at his ear, which tickled dreadfully, and began to cry, whereupon the chief and the woman

leapt up and began to fuss over him.

"Ask for some daylight," whispered the speck of dust.

So the baby cried for some daylight. The chief picked up a carved wooden box, placed it before the baby, and opened the lid. Inside were seven glowing balls of daylight. The chief took out one of the balls and gave it to the baby. The baby was so delighted with the new toy that all his tears were gone at once.

"Ask for a string to be tied to the ball," whispered the speck of dust in the baby's ear.

And the baby began to cry for a string to be tied to the beautiful ball of daylight.

No sooner had the chief tied a string to the ball and given it to the baby, than the little speck of dust whispered in the baby's ear again.

"Move over to the doorway."

The baby crawled over to the hut's doorway, trailing the ball of daylight on the string, and sat, framed by the arch, with daylight shining brightly all around.

Gradually the baby moved farther and farther out of the house, dangling the ball, right to the very spot where the Crow had left his skin. Quick as a flash, the speck of dust fell out of the baby's ear, picked up the skin, and became the Crow again. The Crow snatched the string from the baby and flew off, carrying away the bright ball of daylight.

The baby began to scream and cry,

and all the villagers came rushing out of their houses. They threw stones at the Crow and tried to shoot him down with their bows and arrows, but the Crow flew off toward the west much too fast for them.

When, at last, the Crow came to the land of the Inuit, he broke off a piece of daylight from the ball over each village that he passed and let it fall. Finally, after much traveling, he reached the village that he had set off from. Then he let go of the string, and all that was left of the ball of daylight fell to the ground and shattered. Shafts of light streamed into all the houses. The villagers rushed out of their houses to thank the Crow for his wonderful gift.

The Crow told the story of how he had stolen the light. And he explained to all the villagers that he had not brought enough light for them to have daylight all the time, but only enough for daylight half the year and that the other half of the year they would have darkness.

"But if I had brought enough daylight for it to be always light," he said, "you would have had as much trouble as you did when it was always dark!"

TRUE OR FALSE?

Which of these facts are true and which ones are false? If you have read this book carefully, you will know the answers.

1. Summer falls between May and July at both poles.

2. No plants grow in the polar lands.

3. Plants and animals once lived in a warmer climate on Antarctica.

4. The Arctic was named by the Ancient Greeks after the constellation of the Plough.

5. The Norwegian Roald Amundsen was the first person to reach the South Pole.

6. *The Titanic* sank in 1912 after running into a blue whale.

7. Large fragments from the ice sheet are called bergy growlers.

8. The largest permanent residents on the Antarctic ice sheet are insects.

9. A male Emperor penguin will go as long as four months without food.

10. Polar bear cubs are born two at a time.

11. Arctic people are mostly vegetarian.

12. A car running on gasoline containing lead releases its own weight in carbon dioxide fumes every year.

ANSWERS: 1. False 2. False 3. True 4. False 5. True 6. False 7. False 8. True 9. True 10. True 11. False 12. True

GLOSSARY

● **Baleen whales** have a curtain of bony plates in their mouths. These allow them to sift the tiny krill on which they feed from the ocean.

● **Bergy bits** are large sections that have broken off the icecap.

● **Blubber** is the name for the thick layer of fat on animals such as seals, walruses, penguins, and whales. This layer helps to protect them against the cold. In the past it was used to make goods such as soap and oil for household lighting.

● **Brash ice** is the name for small fragments of ice.

● **Camouflage** is used by animals to hide themselves in their surroundings. For example, the coat of an Arctic fox is white and makes the fox invisible from a distance against the snow. Camouflage helps to protect an animal from predators and helps it to capture prey.

● **Carnivores** are meat-eating animals.

● **Frazil ice** is the first thin ice that forms as the sea begins to freeze.

● **Germination** is the moment when plant seeds come out of their dormant state as a result of suitable conditions for growth and begin to sprout.

● **Glacier** is a river of ice that moves very slowly. It is pushed by new ice that forms on high ground.

● **Greenhouse gases** such as carbon dioxide collect in the earth's atmosphere. They trap the heat rays from the sun and prevent them from bouncing back into outer space. Because of this the earth's climate is changing and growing warmer.

● **Growlers** are small pieces that have broken off the icecap.

● **Herbivores** are plant-eating animals.

● **Iceberg** is a large lump of ice that floats in the sea. Many icebergs break off from glaciers that slowly pour into the sea. Only one-tenth of these icebergs usually show above the surface of the water.

● **Icecap** is a name for the huge shield of ice that covers both the Arctic Ocean and Antarctica.

● **Ice flowers** form when salt is pushed out as the sea freezes. The salt forms strange arrangements of beautiful crystals.

● **Ice sheet** is another name for the Arctic and Antarctic shields of ice.

● **Incubation** is the time between the laying of a bird's egg and its hatching.

● **Meltwater** is the water that appears when ice and snow melt during the polar summer. In some areas meltwater can cause flooding.

● **Nomads** are tribespeople who do not have a settled home. Instead they follow herds of animals in search of fresh pasture. The Lapps of northern Scandinavia travel in this way, tending their reindeer.

● **Ozone layer** prevents the sun's harmful ultraviolet rays from entering the earth's atmosphere. A hole in this layer is forming over each pole, where it is thickest.

● **Pack ice** is formed when slabs of thick sea ice freeze together.

● **Pancake ice** is created when the salt is pushed out of freezing seawater. It often forms in round shapes with raised edges, like pancakes.

● **Pelt** is the name for an animal's fur.

● **Permafrost** is an underground layer of soil that remains frozen all year, even during the polar summer.

● **Plates** are huge sections in the earth's crust on which the continents float. These plates move slowly over hundreds and thousands of years. The continents move with them. As the plates meet and their edges grind against each other, volcanoes erupt and earthquakes occur.

● **Subarctic** describes the area south of the Arctic, which is almost as cold in winter but much warmer in summer.

● **Tabular icebergs** have a large flat surface like that of a table.

● **Toothed whales** have peglike teeth on their lower jaws. The eat animals such as seals, squid, and fish.

● **Tree line** is the farthest point to the north, beyond which the climate is unsuitable for tree growth.

● **Tundra** is the belt of land between the Arctic icecap and the tree line. Rough scrub is the only vegetation here.

INDEX